Contents

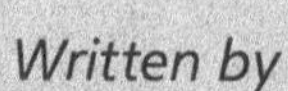

Written by
David Grant

Illustrated by
Dylan Gibson
and **Andy Stephens**

Series editor **Dee Reid**

Part of Pearson

Before reading *Cheat*

Characters

Kris

Kelly

A cleaner

Jake

Tricky words

- lunchtime
- library
- science
- fault
- revised
- grinned
- worried
- whispered

Read these words to the student. Help them with these words when they appear in the text.

Introduction

Kris and Jake are best mates. Kelly is in their year at school. She is a computer genius. Most of the time, Kris and Jake get on well with Kelly but sometimes they are not sure about what she is up to on her computer. One day, Kris and Jake were in the school library. Kris had failed a science test and was worried about what his mum was going to say. Then Jake had an idea to trick Kelly into helping Kris.

It was lunchtime.
Kris and Jake were in the school library on the computers.
"I can't believe I failed my science test," said Kris.
"My mum will kill me when she sees my report."

"It's all your fault," said Kris to Jake. "If you hadn't made me play that stupid game on your X-Box for hours, I could have revised for the test."

"I've got an idea," said Jake. "Kelly's really good at computers, isn't she?"
"Yeah," said Kris. "She can do anything on a computer."

"So, she could hack into the school computer and change your grade!" said Jake.
"I don't think she'll want to do that," said Kris.
"I bet I can trick Kelly into helping you," said Jake. "Leave it to me."

Kelly came into the library.
"Hi guys!" she said.

"I bet you can't hack into this computer and make it think you're a teacher," said Jake.
"It's easy," said Kelly.
"Yeah?" said Jake. He grinned at Kris.
"I'll show you," said Kelly.
"Won't we get in trouble?" asked Kris.
"No one will know," said Kelly. "As long as we don't do anything stupid."

Kelly began to type on the computer.
"You just type that in there," she said. "Then you type this stuff here. Now the computer thinks you're a teacher."
"Is that all you have to do?" asked Jake.
"I told you it was easy," said Kelly.

That afternoon, Kris was in his ICT lesson.
While his teacher was busy helping someone else,
Kris tried to do what Kelly had done in the library.
It worked!
The computer thought he was a teacher.

ST STEPHEN'S HIGH SCHOOL

Reports

Science Reports

Maths Reports

English

He opened the program the teachers used to write their reports.
Then he found his science report.
He changed his grade from 'F' to 'A'.
Then he changed what the teacher had written.
Mum will be really pleased when she reads this, he thought.

After school, Kris told Kelly and Jake what he had done.
"You've done **what**?" said Kelly. "You idiot!"
"I'm not an idiot," said Kris. "You should see my science report. It says I'm really clever."

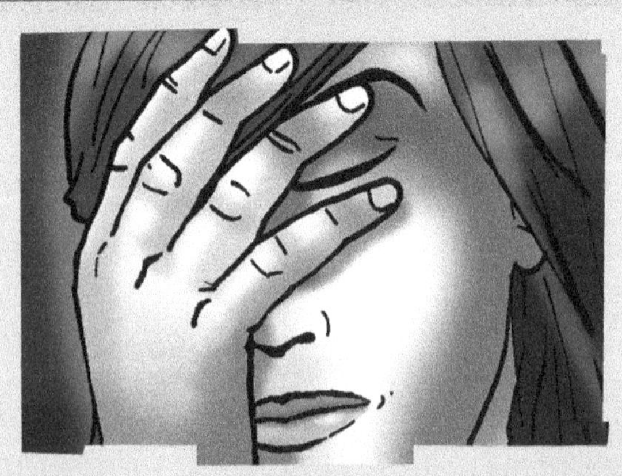

"But they'll know it's been changed," said Kelly.
"And they'll know when it was changed and on what computer. You're going to get in really big trouble."
"Oops," said Kris. He was really worried.
"You've got to help me!" he begged.
"We'd better find a computer," said Kelly.

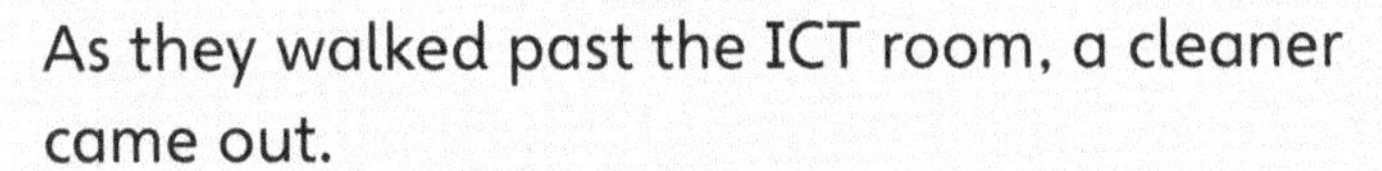

As they walked past the ICT room, a cleaner came out.
He left the door open.
"He'll be back in a minute," said Kelly.
"We'd better hurry. You stay by the door, Jake, and keep a look out."

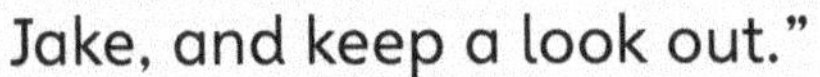

Kelly logged onto a computer.
Jake looked down the corridor to see if anyone was coming.
He heard footsteps.
The cleaner came round the corner.

"Quick!" whispered Jake. "He's coming."
Kelly typed more quickly.
"Hurry up!" whispered Kris.
"I can't get into your report," said Kelly.
"Aha!" said Kelly. "I'm in!"
She hit three buttons and logged off just as the cleaner came in.

“What are you three doing in here?” asked the cleane
“Looking for my scarf,” said Kelly. “Have you seen it?”
“No,” said the cleaner.
“Never mind,” said Kelly. “Maybe I left it in the science lab. Come on, guys.”
Kelly, Kris and Jake left the ICT room.

"Did you do it?" asked Kris.
He looked worried.
"Just in time," said Kelly.
"I had to delete your report but they'll think the computer lost it and write you a new one."

"My mum would have been so happy when she read the science report I wrote," said Kris.

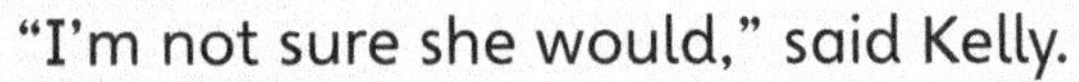

"I'm not sure she would," said Kelly.
"I don't think she'd believe a teacher wrote 'Kris is totally wicked at science'."
"Really?" said Kris.
"No," said Kelly.

Quiz

Text comprehension

Literal comprehension

p4 Who does Kris blame for the fact that he has failed his science test?

p10–11 Why does Kelly think Kris has been an idiot?

Inferential comprehension

p6 How does Jake trick Kelly into helping Kris?

p14 Why does Kelly say she has lost her scarf?

p15 Why does Kelly help Kris to change his report?

Personal response

- Would you like to be able to change reports teachers wrote about you?
- Do you think a pupil could hack into the school report system?

Word knowledge

p4 Find an adjective on this page.

p11 Find a word that means 'pleaded'.

p12 Why is there an apostrophe in the word 'we'd'?

Spelling challenge

Read these words:

thought sure opened

Now try to spell them!

Ha! Ha! Ha!

Why was the computer cold?

It left its Windows open!

Find out about

- White-hat hackers who hack into computers to test how safe they are and black-hat hackers who hack for fun or money.

Tricky words

- commit
- identity
- phreaking
- competition
- arrested
- weapons
- laboratory
- community

Read these words to the student. Help them with these words when they appear in the text.

Introduction

White-hat hackers are paid to break into computers to find problems. Black-hat hackers break into computers for fun or to commit crimes. Some try to steal your identity. Phreaking is hacking into a phone. Kevin Poulsen was a clever phreaker. He used phreaking to win a Porsche car.

White-hat hackers

Hackers are people who break into computers using the internet.
There are two kinds of hackers.
Some people are paid to break into computers, to find problems and to test how safe the computers are. They are called white-hat hackers.

Black-hat hackers

Some people break into computers for fun or to commit crimes.
They are called black-hat hackers.
They never use their real name when they are hacking. They make up hacker names to hide their real identity.
Some black-hat hackers break into computers to steal your identity!

Captain Crunch

The word 'hacker' was first used in America.
A student found out how to hack a phone.
He found that if he re-wired a phone and blew a whistle into it, he could make free phone calls.
He got the whistle free in a packet of cereal called Captain Crunch.
So, people called the hacker Captain Crunch.

Phreaking

Hacking into a phone is called 'phreaking'.
This word comes from the words 'phone' and 'freak'.
Kevin Poulsen was a clever phreaker.
His local radio station had a competition.
People could ring in and try to win a Porsche car.
Kevin used his computer to block all the phone lines.
The only people who could ring the radio station
were him and his friends.

Kevin won the Porsche but he didn't stop there.
He used his computer to commit lots of other crimes.
He was arrested in 1995 and sent to prison for 4 years.
He had to pay a fine of $56,000.

Teenage hackers

In 2002, a 17-year-old boy called Joseph McElroy hacked into the computer network of a top secret weapons laboratory in America. He wasn't trying to get at the secrets. He was just using the power of their huge network to download and store music from the internet.

But then he made the mistake of
telling all his friends.
When they all started to hack into the network,
the people in the laboratory thought it was
a terrorist attack and shut the computer down.
Joseph was given 200 hours of community
service as a punishment.

Many hackers start hacking by breaking into their school's computer network.
In America in 2008 an 18 year old called Omar Khan was charged with hacking into his school's computer network.
It is said that he used teachers' passwords to get into the computer network and change the grades he had been given in school tests.

In one test he had been given an 'F'
because he had been caught cheating.
He changed that grade, and some others,
to 'A' grades.
Omar Khan first appeared in court in 2008
charged with 69 different crimes.
He could go to prison for up to 38 years!

Is your computer safe?

There are lots of different ways a hacker can get into your computer. They can infect your computer with a virus or trick you into downloading a program which will let them in.

How can you tell if your computer has been hacked?

If the hacker has not made changes to your computer then you might never find out that the hacker has been there.

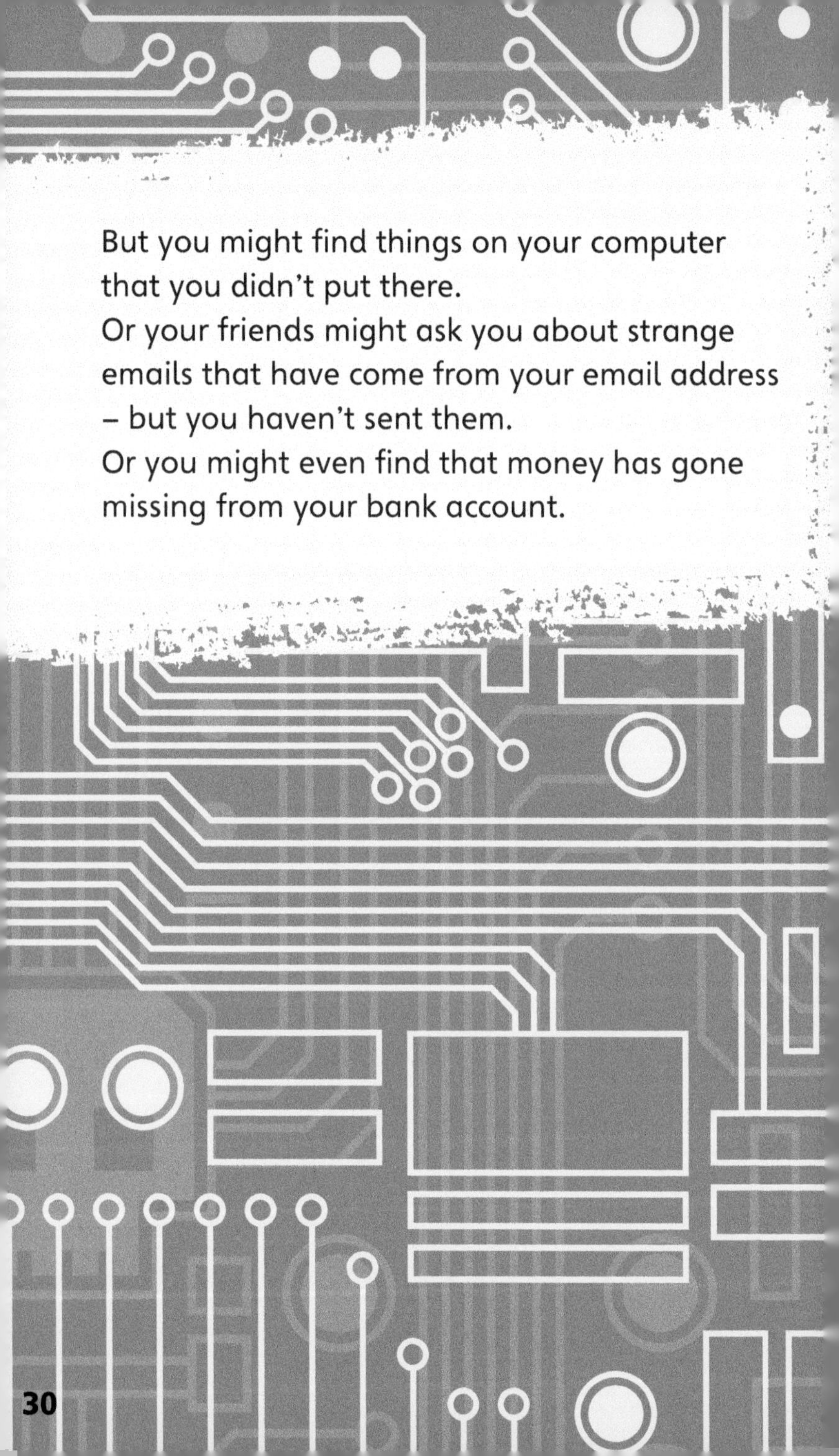

But you might find things on your computer that you didn't put there.
Or your friends might ask you about strange emails that have come from your email address – but you haven't sent them.
Or you might even find that money has gone missing from your bank account.

The best way to stop hackers and keep your computer safe is to have anti-virus software, anti-spyware and a firewall on your computer. You can download these free from the internet.

Quiz

Text comprehension

Literal comprehension

p20 What are black-hat hackers?

p31 What is the best way to keep your computer information safe?

Inferential comprehension

p22 Are hackers clever?

p25 Why was Joseph given community service but not sent to prison?

p30 How might you find out if someone has hacked into your computer?

Personal response

- If you could hack into the school's computer, what would you change?
- Do you think black-hat hackers should be sent to prison?

Word knowledge

p22 Find an adjective.

p26 Why is there an apostrophe after the word 'school'?

p28 Which word connects the two parts of the second sentence?

p30 Find a word that means 'weird'.

Spelling challenge

Read these words: **trying** **people** **haven't**

Now try to spell them!

Ha! Ha! Ha!

Where did the computer go to dance?

To a disc-o!